COLLEGE LONDON PRESS

T0061275

GRADE

01
KEYBOARDS

Published by
Trinity College London Press Ltd
trinitycollege.com

Registered in England
Company no. 09726123

Photography by Zute Lightfoot, lightfootphoto.com

Printed in England by Caligraving Ltd

Parental and Teacher Guidance:

The songs in Trinity's Rock & Pop syllabus have been arranged
to represent the artists' original recordings as closely and
authentically as possible. Popular music frequently deals with
subject matter that some may find offensive or challenging.
It is possible that the songs may include material that some
might find unsuitable for use with younger learners.

We recommend that parents and teachers exercise their own
judgement to satisfy themselves that the lyrics of selected
songs are appropriate for the students concerned. As you
will be aware, there is no requirement that all songs in this
syllabus must be learned. Trinity does not associate itself with,
adopt or endorse any of the opinions or views expressed in
the selected songs.

THE EXAM AT A GLANCE

In your exam you will perform a set of three songs and one of the session skills assessments. You can choose the order of your set list.

SONG 1

Choose a song from this book.

SONG 2

Choose *either* a different song from this book
or a song from the list of additional Trinity Rock & Pop arrangements, available at trinityrock.com
or a song you have chosen yourself: this could be your own cover version or a song that you have written. It should be at the same level as the songs in this book and match the parameters at trinityrock.com

SONG 3: TECHNICAL FOCUS

Song 3 is designed to help you develop specific and relevant techniques in performance. Choose one of the technical focus songs from this book, which cover two specific technical elements.

SESSION SKILLS

Choose *either* **playback** *or* **improvising**.

Session skills are an essential part of every Rock & Pop exam. They are designed to help you develop the techniques music industry performers need.

Sample tests are available in our *Session Skills* books and free examples can be downloaded from trinityrock.com

ACCESS ALL AREAS

GET THE FULL ROCK & POP EXPERIENCE ONLINE AT TRINITYROCK.COM

We have created a range of digital resources to support your learning and give you insider information from the music industry, available online.
You will find support, advice and digital content on:

- Songs, performance and technique
- Session skills
- The music industry

You can access tips and tricks from industry professionals featuring:

- Bite-sized videos that include tips from professional musicians on techniques used in the songs
- 'Producer's notes' on the tracks, to increase your knowledge of rock and pop
- Blog posts on performance tips, musical styles, developing technique and advice from the music industry

JOIN US ONLINE AT:

 /TRINITYROCKANDPOP    @TRINITY_ROCK    /TRINITYROCKANDPOP   and at **TRINITYROCK.COM**

CONTENTS

THE AUDIO

Professional demo & backing tracks can be downloaded free, see inside cover for details.

Music preparation and book layout by Andrew Skirrow for Camden Music Services
Music consultants: Nick Crispin, Chris Walters, Christopher Hussey, Julie Parker
Drums recorded by Cab Grant and Jake Watson at AllStar Studios, Chelmsford
All other audio arranged, recorded & produced by Tom Fleming
Keys arrangements: Nigel Fletcher, Simon Foxley, Imogen Hall, Christopher Hussey, Mal Maddock & Jane Watkins

Musicians
Keys, Bass & Guitar: Tom Fleming
Drums: George Double
Vocals: Brendan Reilly, Bo Walton, Alison Symons

YOUR
PAGE
NOTES

CRAZY
GNARLS BARKLEY

WORDS AND MUSIC: BRIAN BURTON, THOMAS CALLAWAY
GIAN FRANCO REVERBERI
GIAN PIERO REVERBERI

01 GRADE

KEYBOARDS

SINGLE BY
Gnarls Barkley

ALBUM
St Elsewhere

B-SIDE
Just a Thought
Go-Go Gadget Gospel
The Boogie Monster

RELEASED
13 March 2006

RECORDED
2005

LABEL
Warner

WRITERS
Brian Burton
Thomas Callaway
Gian Franco Reverberi
Gian Piero Reverberi

PRODUCER
Danger Mouse

Combining the powerful voice of CeeLo Green and the production expertise of Brian 'Danger Mouse' Burton, the dynamic duo Gnarls Barkley unleashed an instant classic with their debut release 'Crazy' when the song first emerged in 2005.

'Crazy' exploded out of nowhere when it leaked months ahead of the release of Gnarls Barkley's 2006 debut album *St Elsewhere*, and little was known about the song's writers when it first started getting airplay. Based on a piece of music titled 'Last Man Standing' by the Italian composer brothers Gianfranco and Gian Piero Reverberi, written for the soundtrack to the 1968 Spaghetti Western film *Django, Prepare a Coffin*, 'Crazy' became the first single to reach No. 1 in the UK based on download sales alone. It went on to top the charts for nine weeks, becoming the biggest selling song of the year. In the US it spent seven weeks at No. 2, never making the top spot but going on to sell over 3 million copies there. *Rolling Stone* magazine named it their song of the year.

⚡ PERFORMANCE TIPS

There are many different chords in this song, which is presented here in an accompaniment arrangement. Practise the chord changes carefully, keeping the right hand smooth and a steady rhythm in the left hand. This version works fine on piano, but you might also like to experiment with an electric piano sound and even a strings sound for the right-hand melody in the chorus if your instrument is capable of this.

CRAZY

WORDS AND MUSIC:

BRIAN BURTON, THOMAS CALLAWAY
GIAN FRANCO REVERBERI, GIAN PIERO REVERBERI

But think twice,_____ that's my on - ly ad - vice._

D.S. al Coda   Coda   freely

Mm - ah,

oo_____   oo_____   oo_____   oo_____

oo - mm._____

SINGLE BY
The Black Keys

ALBUM
El Camino

RELEASED
6 December 2011 (album)
25 February 2012
(single)

RECORDED
2011, Easy Eye Sound
Studio, Nashville,
Tennessee, USA

LABEL
Nonesuch

WRITERS
Dan Auerbach
Patrick Carney
Brian Burton

PRODUCERS
Danger Mouse
The Black Keys

TECHNICAL FOCUS

GOLD ON THE CEILING THE BLACK KEYS

WORDS AND MUSIC: DAN AUERBACH, PATRICK CARNEY
BRIAN BURTON

Formed in Akron, Ohio in 2001, American blues-infused duo The Black Keys are Dan Auerbach (guitar/vocals) and Patrick Carney (drums). Since their debut release in 2002 they have become one of America's biggest rock bands, notably in their second decade with the US top-five hit albums *Brothers*, *El Camino* and *Turn Blue*.

The Black Keys' seventh album, 2011's *El Camino*, was the duo's first top-ten album in the UK and a No. 2 hit in their native America. Following 'Lonely Boy' as its second single, 'Gold on the Ceiling' features producer co-writer Brian 'Danger Mouse' Burton (no stranger to duos himself, being one half of both Gnarls Barkley and Broken Bells) on bass and keyboards and was The Black Keys' third No. 1 hit on the US alternative chart. Auerbach described the band's approach:

> I've never been into guitar solos. I really like when every instrument in the band is a rhythm instrument. This record has a lot of that going on.

The album earned the band a Grammy for Best Rock Album and a Brit Award for Best International Group. At another awards ceremony, the 2012 MTV Movie Awards, The Black Keys played 'Gold on the Ceiling' accompanied by film star Johnny Depp on additional guitar.

TECHNICAL FOCUS

Two technical focus elements are featured in this song:

* Swing rhythm
* Coordinating ties over the bar line

The opening left-hand pattern, which continues with variations throughout the song, is in a **swing rhythm**. This is a challenge at the specified tempo, requiring stamina and a strong sense of swing feel. Later, there are several places where **coordinating ties over the bar line** becomes a challenge, for example in bars 15–16, 17–18 and 19–20. In these places, make sure that the bass line continues in the left hand while the tie is held in the right hand. Synth or electric piano, if available, would be suitable sounds for this song.

TECHNICAL FOCUS

GOLD ON THE CEILING

WORDS AND MUSIC: DAN AUERBACH
PATRICK CARNEY, BRIAN BURTON

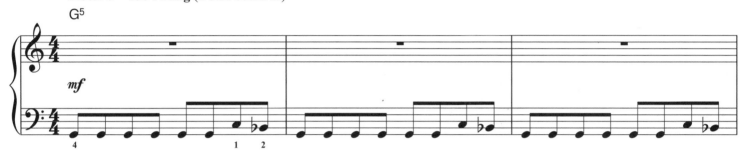

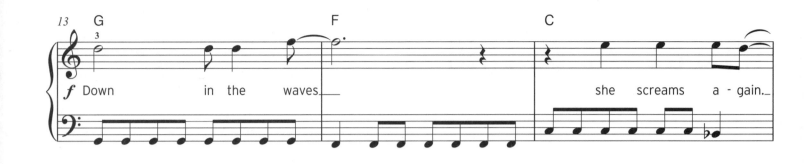

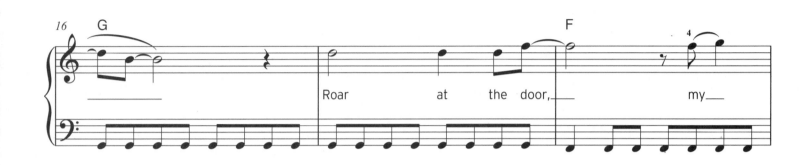

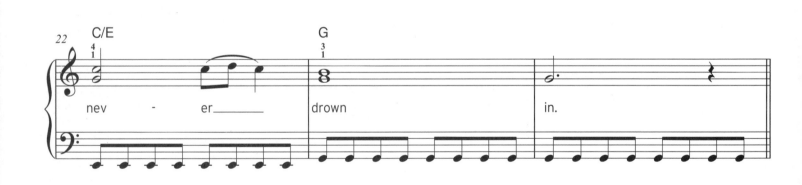

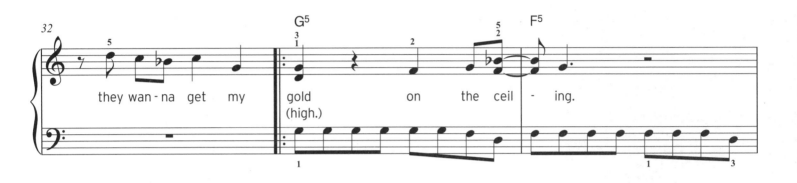

they wan - na get my gold on the ceil - ing.
(high.)

I ain't blind; just a mat - ter of

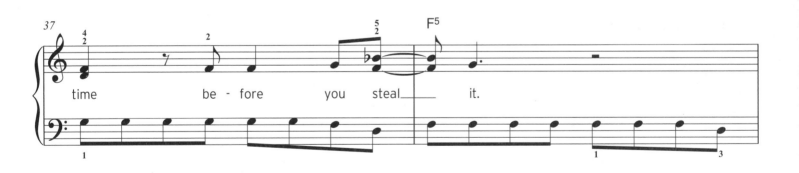

time be - fore you steal it.

It's al - right, ain't no guard - ing my high.

SINGLE BY
The Beatles

B-SIDE
Revolution

RELEASED
26 August 1968

RECORDED
31 July–2 August 1968
Trident Studios
London, England

LABEL
Apple

WRITERS
John Lennon
Paul McCartney

PRODUCER
George Martin

HEY JUDE
THE
BEATLES

WORDS AND MUSIC: JOHN LENNON, PAUL MCCARTNEY

Formed in Liverpool, England in 1960, The Beatles ten-year span saw them become the most successful and acclaimed group in music history. The quartet of John Lennon, Paul McCartney, George Harrison and Ringo Starr still hold the record in the US for the most No. 1 singles (20) and the most No. 1 albums (19). In the UK they hold the record for the most No. 1 albums with 15.

Originally conceived by McCartney with the lyric 'Hey Jules' and intended to comfort Lennon's five-year-old son Julian as his parents were divorcing, 'Hey Jude' was released in August 1968 as a standalone single with Lennon's 'Revolution' as the B-side. It was the first release on the band's newly formed Apple label and was their longest-running No. 1 in the US, where it held out for nine weeks. In the UK it topped the charts for two weeks before being replaced by Apple's second release, Mary Hopkins' 'Those Were the Days' (produced by McCartney). In 2002, Julian Lennon said of being the inspiration for 'Hey Jude': 'It surprises me whenever I hear the song. It's strange to think someone has written a song about you. It still touches me.' In 2015, a UK TV show titled *The Nation's Favourite Beatles Number One* ranked 'Hey Jude' in pole position in a vote by viewers.

 **PERFORMANCE TIPS**

This arrangement features a classic piano accompaniment style where the right hand leads and the left hand follows with offbeat quavers. Watch out for the time signature variation (bars 19–20) and practise crossing your right-hand thumb underneath, which will be needed for the rising melody in bars 29–30. Piano is the appropriate sound for this song.

HEY JUDE

WORDS AND MUSIC:
JOHN LENNON, PAUL McCARTNEY

YOUR
PAGE
NOTES

HOLD ON
ALABAMA SHAKES

WORDS AND MUSIC: BRITTANY HOWARD

SINGLE BY
Alabama Shakes

ALBUM
Boys & Girls

RELEASED
6 February 2012

RECORDED
2011
The Bomb Shelter,
Nashville, Tennessee,
USA

LABEL
ATO (USA)
Rough Trade (UK)

WRITER
Brittany Howard

PRODUCERS
Andrija Tokic
Alabama Shakes

Alabama Shakes are a blues-rock quartet from Athens, Alabama. Led by powerhouse vocalist and guitarist Brittany Howard, the band also includes Heath Fogg on guitar, Zac Cockrell on bass and Steve Johnson on drums. 'Hold On' was the band's first single, and the opening song on their 2012 debut album *Boys & Girls*. The album reached No. 3 in the UK and No. 6 in the US, earning the band three Grammy nominations and the main support slot on a number of US tour dates with one of their heroes, Jack White.

With a gritty mix of soul, blues and rock, Alabama Shakes' exhilarating live performances and Howard's stand-out star quality helped ensure the band's swift ascent. *Rolling Stone* named 'Hold On' as No. 1 in its '50 best songs of 2012' list, likening Howard's singing to 'a husky moaning-in-the-moonlight drawl'.

⚡ PERFORMANCE TIPS

Listen carefully to the style of the bass in the original version of this song and try to replicate the same articulation in your left hand at the opening. Go for a similarly detached style with the repeated quavers that start at bar 9 – these should have a strong ringing quality but without banging. Observe the rests in the section from bar 21 and, for stylistic authenticity, play on an acoustic piano or a digital instrument with piano sound.

HOLD ON

WORDS AND MUSIC: BRITTANY HOWARD

Blues rock ♩ = 88 (2 bars count-in)

Bless my heart, bless my soul; didn-n't think I'd make it to twen-ty-two years old. There must be some - one___

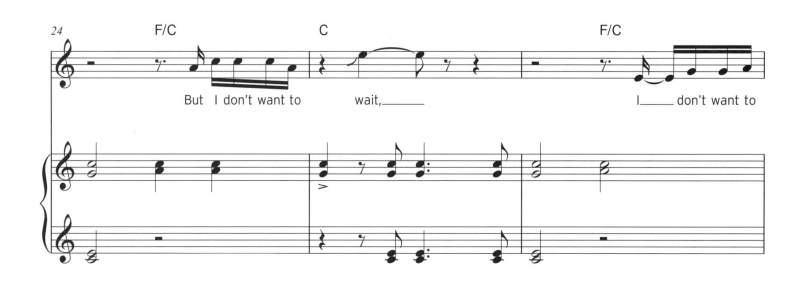

TECHNICAL FOCUS

LE FREAK CHIC

WORDS AND MUSIC: BERNARD EDWARDS, NILE RODGERS

SINGLE BY
Chic

ALBUM
C'est Chic

B-SIDE
Savoir Fair

RELEASED
10 July 1978

RECORDED
1 Januery 1978

LABEL
Atlantic

WRITERS
**Bernard Edwards
Nile Rodgers**

PRODUCERS
**Bernard Edwards
Nile Rodgers**

Fellow session musicians Nile Rodgers (guitar) and Bernard Edwards (bass) formed Chic with drummer Tony Thompson, which by 1978 also included female vocalists Alfa Anderson and Luci Martin. One of the most successful acts of the disco era, their influence extended to hip-hop (sampled on 'Rapper's Delight'), 80s pop (Blondie, Queen, Madonna, Bowie) and electronic dance music (Modjo, Daft Punk).

'Le Freak' was the first single from Chic's second album, 1978's US and UK top-five hit *C'est Chic*. The song was conceived on New Year's Eve 1977 after Rodgers and Edwards were refused entry to New York's famous Studio 54 nightclub. The venue is referenced in the song's lyrics ('Come on down to 54') and it proved to be an immediate club hit. Their third single and third consecutive top-ten hit in the UK (following 'Dance, Dance, Dance (Yowsah, Yowsah, Yowsah)' and 'Everybody Dance'), it remains a dancefloor anthem to this day. It remains Atlantic Records' best-selling single ever, with worldwide sales in excess of seven million copies.

TECHNICAL FOCUS

Two technical focus elements are featured in this song:

- Semiquaver riff
- Staccato

The **semiquaver riff** that appears in bars 10, 18, 46 and 54 requires crisp articulation and rhythmic accuracy. You may find it helpful to practise A minor pentatonic scales to familiarise yourself with this pattern of notes. **Staccato** is a feature throughout in the rising quaver motif that crosses the bar line (for example, the very first two notes of the song). You'll need to keep the same staccato feel even when a chord is held at the same time, for example at bar 5. You could try an electric piano sound in this song, with strings in the right hand if this is possible on your instrument.

LE FREAK

WORDS AND MUSIC:

BERNARD EDWARDS, NILE RODGERS

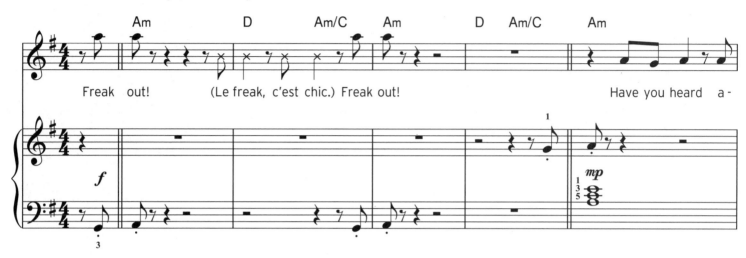

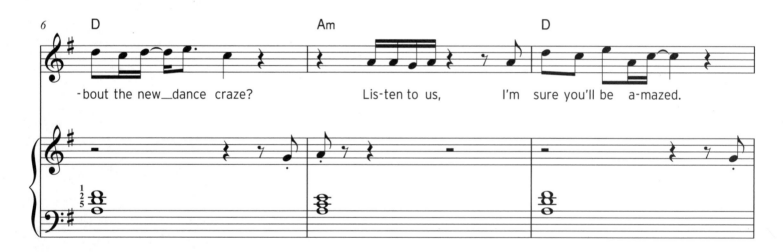

All that pres-sure   got you down?__   Has your head   spin-ning all a-round.

Feel the rhy - thm,   chant the rhyme,__   come on a-long__   and

YOUR
PAGE
NOTES

LOVE IS THE DRUG
ROXY MUSIC

WORDS AND MUSIC: BRYAN FERRY, ANDY MACKAY

SINGLE BY
Roxy Music

ALBUM
Siren

B-SIDE
Sultanesque

RELEASED
September 1975

RECORDED
Summer 1975

LABEL
EG

WRITERS
Bryan Ferry
Andy Mackay

PRODUCER
Chris Thomas

Roxy Music were a hugely influential and commercially successful art rock band who made an instant impact with their debut single 'Virginia Plain' in 1972 at the onset of glam rock mania. Fronted by Bryan Ferry and initially featuring Brian Eno on synthesizer, Roxy Music produced ten UK hit singles over the next decade.

Written by Roxy Music's saxophone and oboe player Andy Mackay with lyrics and vocal line by Ferry, 'Love is the Drug' was the lead single and opening track on the band's fifth album, 1975's *Siren*. The single reached No. 2 in the UK (kept off the top spot by a reissue of David Bowie's 'Space Oddity') and was also the band's first (and biggest) hit in the US. Grace Jones covered the song for her 1980 *Warm Leatherette* album, and Ferry later reinterpreted the song in a 1920s jazz style for the soundtrack to Baz Luhrmann's 2013 film *The Great Gatsby*.

⚡ PERFORMANCE TIPS

Take care with the rhythm of this song's intro - your left hand replicates the original bass line. You may wish to practise first-inversion chord shapes, which feature in the right hand throughout, to help you to learn this song. At bars 27-28 and 31-32, make sure that the quavers stay rhythmically even as you pass them from hand to hand. You could use an electric piano sound if this is available.

LOVE IS THE DRUG

WORDS AND MUSIC:
BRYAN FERRY, ANDY MACKAY
All Rights Reserved. International Copyright Secured

MUSTANG SALLY WILSON PICKETT

WORDS AND MUSIC: MACK RICE

SINGLE BY
Wilson Pickett

ALBUM
The Wicked Pickett

B-SIDE
Three Time Loser

RELEASED
1966

RECORDED
**1966
FAME Studios
Muscle Shoals
Alabama, USA**

LABEL
Atlantic

WRITER
Mack Rice

PRODUCER
Rick Hall

Gospel-trained, Alabama-born Wilson Pickett started out as lead singer of the Falcons, an R&B vocal group, before signing to Atlantic Records and embarking on a solo career. He hit it big in 1965 with the classic 'In the Midnight Hour'.

'Mustang Sally' was written by Pickett's former Falcons bandmate Sir Mack Rice, who started writing the song as 'Mustang Mama' before Aretha Franklin suggested he change the title to suit the chorus. The song was recorded at FAME studios, a converted tobacco warehouse in Muscle Shoals, Alabama, where Percy Sledge's classic 'When a Man Loves a Woman' was recorded. After Pickett finished his final vocal take, the tape recording the session flew off the reel and broke into pieces. Tom Dowd, the legendary engineer and producer, calmly cleared the room and pieced back together the tape that would become one of the funkiest anthems of the 60s by one of the greatest singers in southern soul history.

⚡ PERFORMANCE TIPS

This keyboard accompaniment part will test your ability to play right-hand thirds. You may want to practise the first two bars of the right-hand part in isolation, as this idea is integral to the song and appears in another position later on (bars 13-16). The left hand often follows the rhythm of the right hand but sometimes does not, so take care to observe the rhythmic detail in both hands throughout. Piano and organ would both be good sounds for this song.

MUSTANG SALLY

WORDS AND MUSIC: MACK RICE

Soul ♩ = 110 (2 bars count-in)

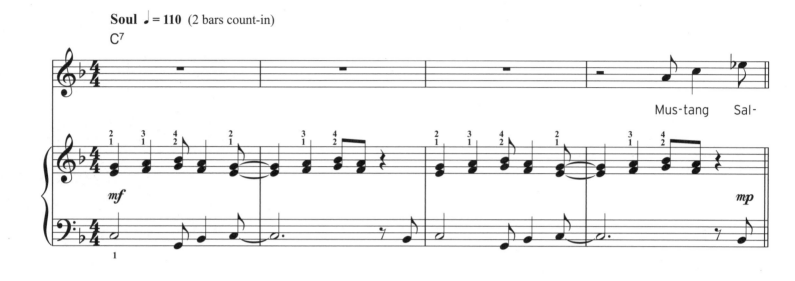

SINGLE BY
Grizzly Bear

ALBUM
Veckatimest

RELEASED
26 May 2009 (album)
1 June 2009 (single)

RECORDED
2008, Allaire Studios,
Ulster County, New York

LABEL
Warp

WRITERS
Ed Droste
Daniel Rossen
Chris Taylor
Christopher Bear

PRODUCER
Chris Taylor

TECHNICAL FOCUS

TWO WEEKS
GRIZZLY BEAR

WORDS AND MUSIC: ED DROSTE, DANIEL ROSSEN,
CHRIS TAYLOR, CHRISTOPHER BEAR

Grizzly Bear are an American band from Brooklyn, New York, comprising multi-instrumentalists Ed Droste (lead vocals, guitar, keys), Daniel Rossen (lead vocals, guitar, keys), Chris Taylor (bass, vocals, woodwind, production) and Christopher Bear (drums, vocals).

'Two Weeks' was the lead single from Grizzly Bear's third album, 2009's *Veckatimest*. Founding member of the band Droste explains how the song came about:

> Chris Bear and I were on a weekend trip to Cape Cod to play around with some song ideas, and that one just came out of nowhere, with Chris starting the piano line and myself quickly following with a vocal melody and lyrics.

Victoria Legrand of the Baltimore band Beach House supplied multi-tracked guest backing vocals on the song, with Rossen explaining: 'When Ed first sent me this demo there was something in the melody that reminded me of Beach House, in a great way. Seemed like a great track for her to sing on.' The song proved to be Grizzly Bear's commercial breakthrough and helped the band score their first top-ten album in the US.

TECHNICAL FOCUS

Two technical focus elements are featured in this song:

- Coordination between hands
- Rhythmic precision

You'll need careful **coordination between hands** in this song, especially in bars 3, 5, 7 and others where isolated left-hand semiquavers will need to be placed accurately in time against the right hand quaver chords. At bars 25-28, you'll need **rhythmic precision** to make sure you that you stay exactly in time with the vocal. Piano is the suggested sound for this song.

TWO WEEKS

WORDS AND MUSIC:
ED DROSTE, DANIEL ROSSEN
CHRIS TAYLOR, CHRISTOPHER BEAR

Would you al - ways,_____ may-be

some - times,_____ make it ea - sy?_____ Take your

time;_____

(Oh___ oh___ oh.)_____

CHOOSING SONGS FOR YOUR EXAM

SONG 1

Choose a song from this book.

SONG 2

Choose a song which is:

Either a different song from this book

or from the list of additional Trinity Rock & Pop arrangements, available at trinityrock.com

or from a printed or online source

or your own arrangement

or a song that you have written yourself

You can play Song 2 unaccompanied or with a backing track (minus the keyboard part). If you like, you can create a backing track yourself (or with friends), add your own vocals, or be accompanied live by another musician.

The level of difficulty and length of the song should be similar to the songs in this book and match the parameters available at trinityrock.com

When choosing a song, think about:

- Does it work on my instrument?

- Are there any technical elements that are too difficult for me? (If so, perhaps save it for when you do the next grade)

- Do I enjoy playing it?

- Does it work with my other songs to create a good set list?

SONG 3: TECHNICAL FOCUS

Song 3 is designed to help you develop specific and relevant techniques in performance. Choose one of the technical focus songs from this book, which cover two specific technical elements.

SHEET MUSIC

If your choice for Song 2 is not from this book, you must provide the examiner with a photocopy. The title, writers of the song and your name should be on the sheet music. You must also bring an original copy of the book, or a download version with proof of purchase, for each song that you perform in the exam.

Your music can be:

- A lead sheet with lyrics, chords and melody line

- A chord chart with lyrics

- A full score using conventional staff notation

PLAYING WITH BACKING TRACKS

All your backing tracks can be downloaded from soundwise.co.uk

- The backing tracks begin with a click track, which sets the tempo and helps you start accurately

- Be careful to balance the volume of the backing track against your instrument

- Listen carefully to the backing track to ensure that you are playing in time

- Keyboard players should not use auto-accompaniment features for these exams as the aim is to play with a backing track

If you are creating your own backing track, here are some further tips:

- Make sure that the sound quality is of a good standard

- Think carefully about the instruments/sounds you are using on the backing track

- Avoid copying what you are playing in the exam on the backing track – it should support, not duplicate

- Do you need to include a click track at the beginning?

COPYRIGHT IN A SONG

If you are a singer, instrumentalist or songwriter it is important to know about copyright. When someone writes a song they automatically own the copyright (sometimes called 'the rights'). Copyright begins once a piece of music has been documented or recorded (eg by video, CD or score notation) and protects the interests of the creators. This means that others cannot copy it, sell it, make it available online or record it without the owner's permission or the appropriate licence.

COVER VERSIONS

- When an artist creates a new version of a song it is called a 'cover version'

- The majority of songwriters subscribe to licensing agencies, also known as 'collecting societies'. When a songwriter is a member of such an agency, the performing rights to their material are transferred to the agency (this includes cover versions of their songs)

- The agency works on the writer's behalf by issuing licences to performance venues, who report what songs have been played, which in turn means that the songwriter will receive a payment for any songs used

- You can create a cover version of a song and use it in an exam without needing a licence

There are different rules for broadcasting (eg TV, radio, internet), selling or copying (pressing CDs, DVDs etc), and for printed material, and the appropriate licences should be sought out.

YOUR
PAGE
NOTES

YOUR
PAGE
NOTES

YOUR
PAGE
NOTES